Living Past the Pain

by

Helen R. Richmond

Published by Divine Destiny Ministries, P.O. Box 832038, Stone Mountain, GA., 30083

Printed in the United States of America

Visit our website:
www.divineconnectionstoday.info
email: hrr87@bellsouth.net

ISBN 978-1-4357-4226-0

Roscoe & Helen: Hawaii 2005

About the Author

Helen R. Richmond is happily married to Roscoe T. Richmond, Jr. and currently resides in Stone Mountain, Georgia. They are both ordained ministers. Additionally, Helen is a mother, grandmother and great grandmother at the tender age of 62. She has taught at Spelman College and Georgia Perimeter College. She is currently an associate minister at Living Faith Christian Ministries and a substitute teacher for the Dekalb County School System. God has blessed her with good health and a good life, despite the hardships delineated in this book.

Acknowledgements

I would first like to acknowledge God as the head of my life. Without God, I can do nothing. God gave me the vision to write the book and I believe it will accomplish what it is set out to do—heal hurting people, in general, and women in particular.

Secondly, I would like to acknowledge my parents, Rev. Owen L. Carter, Sr. and Mrs. Charlotte L. Carter. They trained me up in the way that I should go, even though it took me a long time to return to that training. They gave me the foundation that I needed to get through those difficult times in my life. God has truly blessed both of them with long-life. They are 96 and 89 respectively.

Thirdly, I would like to acknowledge my granddaughter, Alycia N. Edwards. God has given her many talents, one of which is art. She so graciously consented to designing the cover of my first book. Even though we ended up going another route, I am grateful that she would even consider designing the cover for me. Hopefully she will design my next book cover.

Rev. & Mrs. Owen L. Carter, Sr.
1986
50 Years of Marriage
Dad: age 75; Mom: age 68

Alycia N. Edwards
9th Grade, 11/07

Alycia is very dear to me because I have raised her since she was a baby. I have watched her develop into a beautiful young lady, who loves God. Alycia is a straight "A" student in the 9th grade. At age 12 without studying, she scored 1220 on the SAT. One of her desires is to become an engineer. Any college would be privileged to have her as a student. I certainly feel privileged to have her as a granddaughter. As I continue to be a positive influence in her life, I pray that she will not have to experience any type of abuse.

Fourthly, I would like to thank my church family, Pastor Arlene Robie and Living Faith Christian Ministries, who encouraged me along the way. They even prayed over my bound manuscript.

I would also like to thank Chan, the worker who bound my first two manuscripts. The equipment wasn't favorable that day, but she diligently and tenaciously kept to the task at hand to complete it successfully.

Finally, I would like to thank Shanti Roundtree. Shanti and I have been friends for 14 years. We met at a summer program in Massachusetts, when I was pursuing my undergraduate degree. After graduation, we continued to interact at a yearly summer program for Mellon graduate students. Even though Shanti is young enough to be my daughter, we became good friends. She has encouraged me throughout this process, letting me know that I had a great story to tell and could tell it in a way that would be comforting to anyone who would read it. That was a great compliment coming from Shanti, because she is a talented writer, herself. This has been a grueling process, but she never gave up on me. After almost five years, "it is finished!"

Preface

The Spirit of the Lord God is upon me because the Lord has anointed me to preach good tidings to the poor; He has sent me to heal the broken hearted; to proclaim liberty to the captives; and the opening of the prison to those who are bound; . . . To comfort all who mourn ...." (Is. 61:1-2)

God has called me forth to teach, train and mentor women. Of course, I will focus on winning souls to Christ (both male and female), but my specific calling is to women. I have a story to tell that will encourage many women who are suffering from abuse, neglect, abandonment, and other discouraging situations. Many years ago, God delivered me from such a life and is prompting me to share my story, thus, this book.

I have been grappling with this assignment (from God) since 2003. It is very painful writing about difficult times in one's life, but God gave me the strength. My prayer is that you will read my story and be encouraged to do what it takes for you to have an abundant life. After all, "...Jesus came that you may have life more abundantly." (John 10:10)

Dedication

This book is dedicated to all women, especially those who have struggled through a life of pain and suffering--not just normal pain and suffering, but pain and suffering stemming from bad relationships, abuse and a series of bad decisions.

Specifically, I dedicate this book to my daughter, Angel Phillips, my daughter-in-law, Angela Robinson-Carter, and all the other women in my family and circle of friends. I would like for my 13 granddaughters and 1 great granddaughter to benefit from this book, as well.

In fact, I hope that all young girls benefit from this book. Hopefully a responsible female adult would read the book with them or share this information with them to help them realize the importance of making good decisions. Surprisingly, too many teenage girls are experiencing some type of abuse from those who profess to love them. My prayer is that this book would raise an awareness of how abuse occurs and help to eliminate that abuse.

Men could also benefit from this book if they carefully consider the abusive experiences shared in it. Prayerfully they will educate themselves and other men to help end the cycle of abuse toward women and girls that pervades our society.

Table of Contents

Introduction

Living Past the Pain: Reflections of the Past is a "reader friendly" book, intentionally written in a conversational tone.

The book depicts portions of my life through a series of significant events which helped shape me into who I am today. My story is filled with pain and suffering. Sometimes I did not know if I would live or die. Sometimes I thought I had died and gone to hell. Other times things seemed great. Overall, my story will encourage women from all walks of life. If you are going through difficult times of any type, but especially due to any kind of abuse, my story will encourage you. After getting past the pain, there is a happy outcome. Although my life continues to unfold, the pain from the past is gone, and I am looking towards a bright future. All things are possible, if you only believe. I stepped into my divine destiny, and God delivered me from the pain and suffering.

Chapter One
"In the Beginning"

I've been told that I was born on August 16, 1945, a few days before the end of World War II: what an interesting environment in which to enter the world, one of turmoil and despair. Not only was I born into an atmosphere of turmoil and despair, but it was also during a time of racial tension. I was born in Dayton, Ohio, a small town that had very few great opportunities for black people (of course it was Negro at that time). Moreover, my mother, Charlotte L. Carter, looked white and my dad, Owen L. Carter, Sr., was unmistakably a black man. That fact seemed to raise eyebrows whenever my mother would continue to the back of the bus with my father.

Helen: 6 Months Old

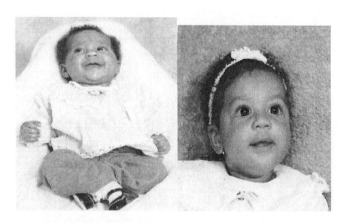

Angel: 4 Months Old   Alycia: 4 Months Old

Get the Picture?

Nevertheless, I made my debut into the world. I remember very little about Dayton, Ohio because we moved to Cincinnati, Ohio when I was four years old. I remember it as if it were yesterday. Our address was 918 Findlay Street. It was a place of meager accommodations, a two-room flat with a bathroom to share in the hallway. There were six children, plus mom and dad, so we lived in pretty tight quarters. Obviously, we were considered poor, but there was a lot of love in our home. We never went hungry, either.

One of my cherished memories is when my mother took me with her on the trolley to go shopping for a dress for my fifth birthday. I can almost see the dress in my mind, but memory of the specifics has faded over time. I do remember the color. It was light green and white. I don't know why that memory sticks with me. I guess it was the excitement of going with my mother and riding the trolley. Perhaps, the most exciting part was getting a new dress because funds were always scarce.

Even though we lived in tight quarters, we had lots of fun. We were one of the first families on the street to get a television. Many of our friends would come over and we would watch television together. Everyone wanted to come to our home because of the television. Things were different back in those days. People were friendlier and neighbors were true neighbors. We also had the opportunity to go play with our friends at their homes. The meager lifestyle did not hinder the fun that I was having at that time.

I don't remember this incident, but my sister told it to me. When I was born, my birth certificate had "white" on it. I assume it was because my mother looked white and the person filling out the papers didn't bother to ask her race. So, when I was ready to go to school, my sister had to take me. They almost didn't let me start that day because of my birth certificate. My sister said they kept asking her if I were white. My sister replied, "No she's not white. Does she look white? I am light-skinned, but my sister really looks white. So she was having a hard time convincing the authorities that I was not white. They finally allowed me to enroll in school.

One last memory during my first five years of life is the day I didn't go to school when I was supposed to go. I was walking to school, which was only about three blocks from our home. I saw one of my friends playing in her yard. I went and joined her. My brother, who was only four and not in school, came down the street eating some grapes. I asked him for some of his grapes. He replied, "Go get your own grapes." I went home to ask my mother for some grapes. She was mopping the floor. She asked me why I was not in school. I told her, very innocently that I was playing with my friend in her yard. I wasn't trying to be funny. I just didn't know the seriousness of what I had done-played "hooky." In my mind, my friend wasn't in school, so why should I go. It was an innocent mistake.   Nevertheless, my mother grabbed me and gave me one of the few whippings that I would get throughout my childhood.

Chapter Two
"Bad Decisions"

It is interesting that I remembered when I was five years old, but the only significant thing that I remember about my life from age six through eleven is getting baptized. My father is a preacher. So I am a "PK" (preacher's kid). Yes, I was raised in the church and could not wait until I was grown so I could stop going. My father started a house-church in the home of our landlord. I remember pretending to pray and shout. We were kids. I was about seven and really didn't understand the concept of salvation. I do remember that we were Pentecostal—the ones who believe in tarrying for the Holy Ghost. I did get baptized when I was seven years old. In retrospect, I am glad that I was trained up in the church. When I was older, I returned to my Christian roots.

More significant was the impact of

moving around many times. Just when I would begin to make friends, I would have to change schools. I was always sad when we moved to a different neighborhood. However, we were never homeless, so I should not complain. I do remember my junior high school years. That is when I fell in love with Ellis; well it was probably puppy love, but you couldn't tell me that then. Ellis and I did everything together. He was very nice to me. As strict as my father was, he allowed me to go to the movies with Ellis when I was in the ninth grade. Before then, I would go to his house all of the time. There were several of the kids in the neighborhood that would always go to his house, so it wasn't anything unusual. My father just didn't know that I called myself "going with" Ellis. We would also hang out over to Andrea's house. I spent a great deal of time there. Her mother worked at night and her dad was never at home, so we had plenty of time to do whatever we wanted to do. People thought

Ellis and I would grow up and get married. I thought we would grow up and get married. It didn't happen.

When I got to high school, I had moved to a different school district. Ellis and I went to different schools. I began to mingle with other people and started liking different boys. I finally broke up with Ellis. He said that I broke his heart. I didn't mean to, but I felt that I had out-grown him. I would have probably been better off with Ellis. I probably would not have gotten pregnant when I was only sixteen years old. However, I didn't stay with Ellis, and I did get pregnant when I was sixteen years old. I had my first child at seventeen.

I had fallen "head over heels" in love with Charles. He was "fine" (lust of the eye) and the star basketball player at Withrow High School, (pride of life). He barely knew that I was alive. Then one night, he offered me a ride home from a basketball game. Another couple was with him and he said we would ride around and have some fun. Of course, I could not resist. I mean, I just told you that I was head over heels in love with him. Finally, he noticed me. It was a cold January night. Sitting in the back of the car, we had sex and I got pregnant. Yes, it only took one time. Later, I remember feeling like I was about to have my cycle, but it never came. I panicked.

How could that have happened to me? I was scared. What would my mother and father think, especially my father? I mean my father was a pastor. He had been extremely strict. I had a sister who had already had a baby before she was married. What shame this would bring on my father and mother.

I was able to hide it for a long time. When I finally got up enough nerve to tell my sister, the one who had already had a baby, she told me to tell my mother. I finally did tell her and she said that she already knew it. I would pretend to have my cycle, but she said she would check behind me and knew I was faking.

Yet, she did not come to me; she waited until I told her. She was quite supportive, but my dad "hit the roof." He threatened to put me out of the house, and I decided to drop out of school.

In those days, it wasn't easy to go to school while pregnant. They scorned you for being pregnant and not married. Yet, I was so close to the end of my junior year, I changed my mind and decided to go back and finish out the year. I tried to cover up my pregnancy, but people knew. Ugly rumors spread and Charles was long gone. I was in it by myself. My so called friends abandoned me. Nevertheless, I made it through to the end of the year. I only needed one class to graduate, but no one made any effort to allow me to get that extra course and graduate a year early. I would graduate a year late in 1964 instead of 1963.

Not only was I discouraged about the pregnancy, but I was disappointed that I had to drop-out of the Minstrels. Minstrels were a big talent show that Withrow High School had every spring. It was a really prominent production and everyone wanted to be a part of it. I had tried out for the chorus line. Today they call it the dance team. I made the chorus line, along with only one other black person, another girl. I was elated. Finally I could dance. I had always had the desire to dance, but because of my father's strict religious beliefs, he would never allow me to take dance lessons, even from my sister who was a natural dancer. At age sixteen, I was determined I would make the chorus line and finally dance. Surprisingly, my father put up no opposition, which made what happened even more devastating. Once the school found out that I was pregnant, I was told that I could no longer perform with the Minstrels. They said that it was a safety issue and they could not be responsible if I were to get hurt. The bottom line was that my dream was crushed. I would not be able to continue to dance. I still remember the basic dance routine and the song. The name of the song was

"Surrey with a Fringe on Top." During the routine, we would end up building a surrey (carriage) with our bodies and umbrellas. The colors were pink and black. I'm sure you understand how disappointed I was because of the fact that I remember all of the details. Nevertheless, I blame no one but myself. Yes, I tried to blame Charles and the school, but in the end it was my bad decision which got me into the predicament. Things did get better, though.

Over time, my father accepted the fact that I was pregnant. Obviously, he did not put me out of the house. I had an uncomfortable pregnancy, plagued with morning sickness and back discomfort. I gained thirty pounds during this pregnancy. I only weighed 96 pounds before I got pregnant, so the extra weight played a role in my discomfort. Fortunately, I began to be excited about the fact that a baby was on the way, and I began to prepare for the baby. Of course, back then, you couldn't get a test to see if it would be a boy or girl, so I had to wait until the end. I did, however, begin to buy baby clothes, etc. I even bought the baby bed before the baby came. As I stated earlier, the father denied being the father, so I had no support from him. His mother helped in a small way, though. Mother's always know. I didn't pursue any legal procedures to determine paternity, either. So when my beautiful baby boy, Terence, was born on September 24, 1962, I got a job and took care of him. No, I didn't get on Welfare.

Even though I was responsible, financially, I had not really learned my lesson about life. I began to go out and stay out late at night. I took for granted that my mother would keep my son for me. In fact, I almost expected it. My mother was a very sweet and mild person. She was always there for me and yes, she did take care of my son. So while I was going out having fun, my mother was raising my son. I was "running wild." I started drinking and going out with a friend of my sister's boyfriend. Drinking distorted my judgment, and needless to say, I got pregnant again. This time, I had planned to give the baby up for adoption. That didn't happen. When my water broke, I barely made it to the hospital before the baby came. I saw everything during the delivery, even the head when it first popped out, and could not bear to give up my beautiful baby boy. I believe it was God's way of allowing me to make the good decision to keep my baby. He was a sweet baby. In contrast to my first son, this one hardly cried and was no trouble at all.

There I was, a mother of two and barely eighteen years old. I was determined to get my diploma, though and slowed down long enough to take the English class that I needed to graduate. I graduated in June of 1964 instead of June of 1963, but I did graduate. I regretted not having had the opportunity to finish school with my class and then go on to college. However, it was the bad decisions that I had made that put me in that predicament. I had no one to blame but myself. I would just say to young girls out there and women, too: "Stay focused on your goals, dreams and aspirations. Don't let your feelings get in the way of good decisions. Look at what happened to me with all of my bad decisions."

Although I had made many bad decisions and I hadn't given my life to the Lord, I believe the Lord was watching over me. Like I said, I never got on Welfare. I worked to earn money for both of my children. I still wanted to party, but I was always financially responsible for the boys. Oh, by the way, my second son, Kevin, was born September 25, 1963, one year and a day after my first son. They were like twins in age, but as different as day and night. I loved both of them, though.

As I stated, I always worked, but I wanted a better job. I had worked at a jewelry store, polishing sterling silver pieces and at a dry cleaner, hanging clothes. I remembered the eleventh grade school counselor telling me that if I ever needed anything, call and he would try to help me. That was after I completed the eleventh grade. He knew that I was pregnant. So, two years later, I called him about a job and he remembered me. He referred me to General Motors Acceptance Corporation (GMAC) and I got my first office job. I was the only black person there, but with my fair complexion, I was not too noticeable. That is probably why they hired me—I blended in with the others. Eventually, the people accepted me and I had wonderful experiences with many of the people at the office. I actually developed several meaningful friendships.

Chapter Three
"The Love of My Life"

Johnny Smith was a photographer. I met him through my sister. She had told him how cute I was and he wanted to take some pictures of me. I was delighted. It always boosts your morale when someone thinks you are photograph material. At least that is how I felt. But before you know it, I was falling in love with Johnny. I only thought I had been in love before, but now it was the real thing. I couldn't keep him off of my mind and I couldn't stay away from him. I remember walking to his house unannounced because I wanted to see him so badly. I was nineteen. Apparently, he liked me, too, because he would never turn me away when I would come unannounced. At that time, he didn't have a telephone, so I couldn't call him. We did have a telephone, but I just couldn't seem to wait for his calls. My uncle once told me that I fell too hard for guys. He suggested that I control my passions. I never

Photo by Johnny Smith

Helen, Age 19

took his advice. I seem to always fall "head over heels" in love.

Johnny was about nine years older than I. He was a smooth operator and I just couldn't seem to stay away from him. He had hooked me and I wanted to be his wife. That wouldn't take place for three years. Prior to getting married, Johnny and I had fun, but we also had rough times. Johnny was a ladies' man. Because he was a photographer, he knew many women. You know how women are. They flaunt their bodies and men respond. I was jealous and never felt secure with him. Soon, he would give me good reason to have those insecure feelings. Nevertheless, when he proposed to me in 1967, I gladly accepted the proposal and we were married on August 26, 1967.

I won't go into all of the details, but our marriage was on the rocks from the beginning, but I just didn't know it. I found out from a reliable source Johnny was involved with another woman. Apparently he had been dating her at the same time that we were dating. She thought he was going to marry her. I don't know why he chose me over her, but from what I understand, they had a serious relationship. "They" say that you shouldn't believe what you hear from others. I agree to a certain extent. However, when a person gives you reason to believe it is true, that's a different story. Johnny gave me many reasons to believe the stories were true. Many things happened and as time went on, we grew farther and farther apart. I finally could not take it any longer and I left him in January of 1970. Our divorce was final in about three months after our separation.

It was a difficult decision for me. I still loved Johnny and my heart was aching. Several months went by and we began to date or at least see each other. Our relationship grew more intense. Yet, there was no sign of any commitment. I finally gave him an ultimatum:

Either we would have a serious relationship and consider remarrying or we would stop seeing each other. He chose the latter. I was devastated. My heart ached for a very long time. It actually took years for me to overcome the devastation. It probably would have taken longer but I met Dwight.

Photo by Johnny Smith

Helen, Age 20

Helen, Age 26

This photo was taken for Dwight. He kept asking me to take a picture for him, but every time I went to his house, it would be in a drawer. I assume he was hiding it from his fiancée. I put up with that, too.

Chapter Four

"Another Bad Decision"

I was lonely, heart-broken, and sad and so on. I was still working at GMAC. Dwight worked for the accounting firm that audited our books. He came gliding down the aisle with his beautiful dark brown eyes, his reddish brown complexion, every hair in place, sharp as a tack and a smile on his face that could melt an igloo in the Antarctic. I was "sprung" from the beginning. Our eyes locked on each other and before you knew it we were flirting with each other.

I told my friend about him. She told me that she knew Dwight and that was it. When we had our first date, I told her about it. She told me more this time. She said that she used to date Dwight, but he was heavily involved with another young lady that he planned to marry. It was too late. I made another bad decision—to keep seeing Dwight. When my friend told me that she used to date Dwight, I thought it was a long time ago. Wrong. In fact, she had seen him since we were dating. I couldn't believe it. Here we were letting a man cause friction in our friendship. But that is how women are sometimes. We allow our emotions to dictate what we should do instead of our minds. What would happen next made me wish that I had taken my friend's advice. Dwight turned out to be a possessive abuser.

Even though he was involved with another young lady (I did find that out), I just couldn't stop seeing him. Yes, you guessed it. We were sexually active. I would spend the night at his house and his other girlfriend would call him on her break. She worked at Delta at night. Anyway, sometimes she would interrupt our sexual encounters with a phone call. Dwight would talk to her like nothing was going on; and I put up with it. What was I thinking? How could I disrespect myself like that? I guess I was just lusting after the flesh.

After a while, I told Dwight I was going to break up with him. He began to threaten me. He was extremely jealous. That is usually the way guys are when they are doing things outside of a relationship. They have to control you, so that you won't find out what they are doing. I wasn't the only other woman, either. I guess, by now, you are wondering what kind of person I am to let men use me like that. I was a woman who felt worthless without a man in her life. I felt that my love for that person should be enough to make them just want me. It hadn't worked that way yet. I was always either the "chick on the side" or there was "a chick on the side." Dwight even took me over to his mother's house. She thought I was the other young lady, because, get this, we even looked alike. He was bold.

I finally got up enough nerve to go over to Dwight's when I knew that his fiancé would be there. I sat out in my car a long time before I could actually go to the door. When I did, bless her heart, she told me that I had to be lying. There was no possible way that Dwight could be seeing me. I even told her that I was there many times when she would call at night. She didn't want to accept it. I don't know what happened after I left, but they eventually got married.

As I stated earlier, Dwight was abusive. One day he came over and I was standing outside talking to my ex-husband, Johnny. Ironically, we lived two doors down from each other. When Dwight and I went into my apartment, he began to beat me. He beat me until my face was swollen and my eyes were black and blue. I had to wear sunglasses to work to try to cover up what had happened. My friend noticed and asked if Dwight had done it. I told her yes. She said, "I told you that he was bad news, but you wouldn't listen." I really wished that I had listened. On several other occasions, Dwight beat me. I finally got up enough nerve to break up with him. I still cared for him, but I didn't love him as much as I had loved Johnny. It was a little easier to break up with Dwight. Part of the reason was that I had met someone else. He would become my second husband. His name was Harold.

Chapter Five

"The Second Time Around"

If I thought that I had loved Johnny, it was nothing compared to the way I felt about Harold. We met at the bowling alley. It was September 11, 1972. His tall stature, beautiful brown skin, curly black hair and domineering voice captured my attention and from that point on, I couldn't get him out of my mind and didn't want him out of my sight. There he stood, the man of my dreams. The feeling was mutual, because we just hit it off right away. In eighteen days, we were married, September 29, 1972: the second time around. By November 30, 1972, we were leaving a snow blizzard in Cincinnati, Ohio and on our way to Atlanta, Georgia. Harold and I would spend seven years of marriage together in Atlanta, Georgia.

When we first moved to Atlanta, we stayed with his sister. She lived in meager conditions with several children of her own. I left my two sons in Cincinnati with my mother until we could get established, but it was still crowded with just the two of us. Nevertheless, they welcomed us with open arms. I got a job first and soon afterwards Harold got a job. In three months, we were able to get our own apartment. It was a very nice place off of Fairington Road. It is now called Lithonia, Georgia, but then, I don't believe it was called Lithonia. Anyway, we lived in a very exclusive complex nestled in the greens of the Fairington Country Club (I don't believe it exists anymore). We were very comfortable and were about to bring the boys to Atlanta.

Once they came, things changed somewhat, but we still had a happy home. Harold was a good provider, but he liked to bowl for money. I liked to bowl, too. After all, that is how we met—bowling. But when it gets to be an obsession, it can cause a strain in any relationship. As I reflect on those days, I see now that I went along with it because I couldn't change it. I had adhered to that saying, "If you can't beat it, join it." It wasn't that bad, though, because I would bowl, too. We went on bowling trips with other people. We founded a bowling club, "The Golden Arms, and won money in tournaments. In fact, my daughter was practically raised in the bowling alley—at least her first four years.

Even though our relationship was good, we had struggles and financial problems, but our love sustained us during those difficult times. Then he decided to form a singing group. At the time, I thought it was a great idea, but it was the beginning of the downfall of our relationship. It was glamorous at first, to sit in the audience while they were performing and know that I was the wife of one of the singers. As time went on, it took its toll on my confidence. Women would flirt with the group right in front of my face. Women are shrewd and will do anything to get what they want. At least that is what I encountered during the entertainment episode of my life with Harold. Men are sneaky. Harold would always say, "Oh that's just the way it is in the entertainment business." Rehearsals began to take him away from home more and more. Then travels out of town that did not include me became more frequent. I could sense that Harold was "messing around" on me, but I couldn't pinpoint it. It was a big mess. There were other women involved, but I chose to stay in the marriage and try to work it out.

Finally, the singing group stopped, and our relationship got better. I got pregnant with my daughter, Angel. She was born September 18, 1975. I had turned thirty on August 16, 1975. She brought a joy in our lives that would help to sustain our relationship for a few more years. There were "bumps in the road," but we began to progress financially. We bought a house in 1978 and things were great. Yet, there was still a sense of insecurity on my part. I found out later that Harold had been seeing other women on his job. He was the manager of a shoe store at Greenbriar Mall. Once, he even left me and stayed with another woman for a short time. We worked things out and he came back home. I was devastated about what had happened, but glad to have him back home. Things never were the same, though. In my spirit, I knew things weren't right, but I tried to hold on as long as I could. Finally, we separated. I asked him to leave and I remained in our house. After he left, I found out that one of the women he had been seeing while he was singing had gotten pregnant by him. Even though we were separated when I found out, it happened while we were together. That really broke my heart into tiny pieces.

I would overcome that devastation by getting involved with a much younger guy. I won't give all of the details, but it was someone whose mother had been a close friend to both Harold and me. We were in a relationship for

44

about a year and he ended up breaking my heart, too. He got involved with someone he met at college. She got pregnant and he stayed in a relationship with her. I hadn't realized that I was so attached to him, but I was. I suffered many days and nights, crying and moping over him. Eventually I got over him, but it was a long hard journey.

As I reflect on all of the relationships I have mentioned, I seemed to have been very weak. It seems that I was willing to put up with anything in order to have a man in my life. When Christ isn't in your life, you're subject to do anything or allow people to treat you any kind of way. I guess hindsight is always 20/20, but if I knew then what I know now, I probably would not have put up with all of the heartaches. Nevertheless, everything that I went through then contributed to my being who I am today.

Chapter Six

" To Hell and Back"

It was a hot summer night back in June of 1981. I was staying with my play mother in Decatur, Georgia. I had just returned to Atlanta from a failed attempt at continuing my education at the University of Georgia. I had met a nice lady on the bus and she had told me that she had a room for rent; it wasn't a boarding house, though, it was a room in her home. She had to get approval from her "old man," as she referred to him. I was up the street with some friends waiting on them to pick me up so we could talk about the living arrangements. To my surprise, only Andrew came to pick me up.

The house was just around the corner, about one-half mile from where I was staying with my play mother. At this time in my life, I was quite an interesting character. I wore short shorts, I weighed 98 pounds, and I was "easy on the eyes." Of course, I was single, not dating anyone, and had just broken up with a much younger man. In essence, I was miserable. When I had met Betsy, she seemed like an older woman. I found out later that she was my age. However, I looked and acted much younger than she did. So when Andrew drove up, I was shocked to see how young and attractive he was. As nature would have it, I immediately began to feel an attraction to him. I tried to contain it, but it was definitely a strong attraction.

Nevertheless, I went to the house and sat down to discuss my living there with Betsy and Andrew. In my mind, I knew this would not be a good situation, but I couldn't help myself. As we talked, I could hear myself subtly flirting with Andrew. Yet, I showed him that I was not one who could be controlled nor go along with anyone's program.

After much discussion, not necessarily about my living there, Andrew approved of me and said it would be okay if I wanted to rent the extra room. We decided on an amount and before long, I was moving in. My play sister tried to talk me out of moving in with them. She could sense that I had feelings for Andrew and told me that it wouldn't be a good idea for me to move in. I ignored her advice and moved in with them anyway.

I couldn't control the way I felt about Andrew. As I stated earlier, he was very attractive. He was also very charming. He seemed to know how to turn on that charm to make himself irresistible. Before I could get a grip on my feelings, I had fallen in love with him. I had no shame about it either.

Andrew started picking me up from work or from some other meeting place. We would go out together and have a wonderful time. I would come home before Andrew, but Betsy was no dumb woman. She began to put two and two together. From what Andrew said, she started asking him questions about me. She wanted to know if we were seeing each other. Apparently, she was accustomed to him "cheating" on her, but I guess I was too close for comfort. One night while I was with Andrew, I spilled my drink in the car. I wet my clothes and the car. When I came home that night, I mentioned that my clothes were wet. The next day when Andrew was taking Betsy to work, he said that she noticed that the car was damp. She asked him if I had been in his car the night before. She told him that I had come home with my clothes wet. Of course, Andrew denied that I was with him, but after that she became very suspicious. Because he was used to having another woman, he knew how to handle the situation. I began to get very uncomfortable with the situation.

By now, I was blinded by my feelings. Andrew and I had become intimate. He knew what to do to make me feel good and I didn't want to share him with anyone. However, I would come to find out that the only way I could be with him would be to share him. That was his lifestyle. He was a "player." I was in too deep now. I could not seem to resist him. So I went along with his program. He continued to live with Betsy, but I moved out. I wanted him to move out, too, but he didn't. He started telling me that as soon as he "got situated," he would move out. I knew he was just leading me on. He didn't even have a steady job at the time. He was with Betsy for a place to stay, and he was with me for a place to play. I would soon regret that I had ever laid eyes on him.

When I left, I went back to my play mother's until I could save enough money to get my own place. I had a decent job now, but it was difficult to save money, because Andrew was always forcing me to give him money. Yes, I had become a victim of abuse. He would threaten to come on my job and embarrass me if

I didn't give him money. When we went out to eat, he never had any money, so I had to pay. As I look back, he had all the characteristics of a man who uses women to get what he wants. After charming them and then being intimate with them, he threatens to leave them if they don't do what he wants. Yes, I had become a part of that vicious cycle. Andrew had "stung" me with his love, and I would suffer from it for years before I would come to my senses.

With Andrew, I went to hell and back. I can't count the number of times he beat me, forced me to have sex, took my money or verbally abused me. I was trapped. I knew it was my fault for being in that situation. I never should have moved in the house with him and Betsy. I am not taking the blame for being abused. I am saying that I went into the furnace knowing that the fire was burning hot. In other words, I brought it on myself by making the worst decision of my life. Once I was in it, it was hard to get out. Andrew was extremely possessive and jealous. I attributed that to the fact that he was messing around. He had to keep tabs on me, so I wouldn't run into him doing whatever he was doing. It's a form of control, too.

Let me give you a detailed account of one of my abusive encounters with Andrew. One night I decided to visit a friend. It got late, so I decided to spend the night. The next day, Andrew was waiting for me in front of my apartment. As we went in, he began to question me about where I had been. When I told him, apparently he didn't believe me. He began to slap me and beat me until I screamed and wreaked with pain. I was helpless. As the beating subsided, he forced me to have sex with him—telling me he beat me for my own good and because he loved me. "If that's love, please keep it, I thought." But I was engrossed with fear and could only respond to his wishes. It was humiliating and sickening, but I was trapped; I even enjoyed it in the end.

Even though I knew that I wasn't the only woman in his life and that he was abusive, I still couldn't seem to leave him. Part of it was because I was afraid, but part of it was because I loved the way he made me feel. I know now that it wasn't love. It was lust. As I stated above, even when he would come to my house, beat me, and then force me to have sex with him, I ended up enjoying it. My flesh wanted to be satisfied, but my heart was aching.

In the midst of all of the abuse, I did something very foolish. I finally got my own place in December of 1981, and I allowed Andrew to stay with me. I guess you would call it staying with me. He was still Andrew. He was still staying with Betsy and me. We were his two women, along with some others whom I didn't know. Betsy told me about the others. I guess she was trying to make me jealous. As I look back, I wonder why I put up with such a lifestyle. It was crazy. I could deal with Betsy, but not the others.

I would try breaking up with Andrew, but he wouldn't leave me alone. After a few days of being away from him, I yearned to feel his touch. I wanted him to come back. Of course, he continued to call me even when we were apart. That made it even more difficult to say "no." As time went on, I began to realize that I would always share him with another woman. I tried to accept that fact, but it was very difficult.

By April of 1983, we moved into another apartment. This time the apartment was in his name. It was a huge mistake. Even though the apartment was in his name, he still didn't want to help pay the rent, etc. I was a fool to continue to be with him. I was a miserable person and poisoned by lust. By now, I had a very good job. I was working for an exclusive office supply company that is no longer in business. I started out as a secretary, but in less than one year, I became an outside sales person. I excelled. I was making big bucks, but I wasn't seeing the fruit of my labor, because Andrew was draining me physically, emotionally and financially. I wasn't happy, either.

If it hadn't been for the situation with Andrew, I could have been one of the happiest people on earth. I had a good job, I was healthy, and I looked good. Nevertheless, the strain from the bad relationship drained the joy out of me. The abuse had begun to happen more frequently. I was afraid to call the police, because from past experience, they do very little. Afterwards, I would be susceptible to more abuse. I seemed to be living in hell with no way to escape.

When I started telling Andrew that I was going to leave, he would threaten to kill me. It was horrifying. It was bad before, but when he started threatening to kill me, I just felt helpless.

I remember one day coming home and for no apparent reason, he started threatening me. He ended up choking me to the point where I couldn't breathe. He said he just wanted to keep me in my place and show me he was the boss. Again, I felt helpless.

As if matters were not already bad enough, Andrew started smoking crack cocaine. He became addicted. Andrew, never really had a steady job for long, but by now, he hardly ever worked. He was busy getting high. For me, the fire in hell got hotter. If you know anything about drug addicts, especially crack cocaine addicts, there is no limit to what they will do for "another hit." Andrew began to stay out all night long. It was a relief for me. I was glad when he was gone, but when he came home, he would often force me to have sex with him. By now, I had begun to dislike it. Even though I was not a Christian, yet, I would pray for deliverance from this evil man. It was truly hell on earth. Not only did he abuse me, but he began to steal things from my home and pawn them so he could buy drugs.

We moved again in the summer of 1983. This time we moved into a house on Glenwood Avenue. It was right down the street from Temple of Faith Church of God in Christ. I wasn't going to church, but I would always wonder about that church. That church will play a prominent role in my life and will be discussed later.

In spite of all of that, Andrew and I got married in October of 1984. What a ridiculous move. Things were no better. I was living with the devil. No matter what I did to try to make things better, they got worse. Once again, I began preparations to leave, but he would follow me and threaten me. My life was a living hell.

I needed a change. In October of 1985, I called my play mother and asked her to take me to church. I told her that I needed to go badly. I hadn't forgotten my roots. I knew church would be a good beginning in my attempt to change my circumstances. She said that if I would come and get her, she would take me to her church. I went to Temple of Faith (the church down the street from the house on Glenwood Avenue) for the first time and gave my life to the Lord. I was forty by then, and my life really did begin once I accepted Christ. However, the situation with Andrew didn't get better.

At first, it appeared that things were better. When he found out that I was going to church, he came to church, too. I had left him, but evidently, he had been following me around, literally stalking me because he knew where I was. He pretended to be sincere about church. He said that he wanted to give his life to Christ, too. He actually came before the church and confessed Christ. I found out later that he would leave church and go smoke crack cocaine. He was only joining the church to appease me—to get me to stay with him. Well, I fell for it. He even joined the usher board. He put on a good act. That is all it was, though, an act. He had not really changed. The crack cocaine raised its ugly head, and Andrew could no longer control his addiction.

If I thought I was living in hell before, the fire was even hotter, now. I thought I had gotten rid of him when I moved in December of 1985. Notice all of the moving in an attempt to get away from Andrew. Moving doesn't help if you don't change your mindset. Up to this point, I hadn't really made up in my mind that I was going to sever all ties.

It was a very nice apartment and I was glad to be away from him. One day I left work and he was outside waiting for me. He said he just wanted to talk. So, I listened. I should have known that he never just wants to talk. There is always an ulterior motive. His motive was to get me back. Yet, I believe it was even more than that. After I allowed him to move in, I found out that Betsy had lost her house, which is where he had continued to live (both places: with her and me). So, he really needed a place to put all of his belongings. I was his only option. Like a fool, I fell for his line and let him come to live with me. By the way, we were still married—if that's what you want to call it. Allowing him to come back was the worst thing I could have ever done.

I don't want to go through all of the disgusting details, but I will share one more incident. By now Andrew was totally strung out on drugs. I was getting ready to go somewhere, when I looked out the patio and saw him climbing up the balcony (I lived on the second floor). I panicked, but had the presence of mind to lock the patio door. It did no good. He kept pulling and kicking it until he opened it. I grabbed my keys, but forgot my purse and ran out of the apartment screaming. By the time I was able to call 911, Andrew had gone with my purse. Of course my purse contained my driver's license and credit cards, some diamond earrings and a gold bracelet. Needless to say, I would never see those things again, except for my driver's license.

I was in the deepest pit of hell. There seemed to be no way out. In the meantime, I moved again, trying to get away from him. In fact, the above incident took place at my new apartment. The verbal, physical and sexual abuse continued. Yes, I was saved, but it seemed like things were worse than they were before I got saved. I cried out to the Lord to help me. It seemed that I was all by myself. At church, I felt very comfortable, but I would dread going home. I literally feared for my life.

Finally, Andrew decided to go into a drug rehabilitation program. I thought that would help. I found out later that he did drugs on his first weekend pass. The program was futile. It was my insurance that paid for it, so I felt like it was a wasted endeavor. Anyway, he didn't complete the program. When he came home, it wasn't long before he was back at it again: the abuse, the drugs, the making my life a living hell.

I began to think about leaving for good. I felt that I would rather be dead than to live like I was living. I began to make preparations to leave. I had made arrangements with a girl friend to move in with her. So one day in January of 1987, I began my exit. My friend came over and helped me with the things I could put in our cars. That weekend, I would have others help me move my things on a truck. It was grueling, but well worth it.

I was finally gone. Yet, I didn't feel totally free. I was still moving about in fear. Would he find me? Would he try to hurt me? Would I ever totally be rid of him? These were just some of the questions floating around in my head. Then one cold January day in 1987, I got some answers.

I was leaving the bank and heading down Martin Luther King, Jr. Drive. All of a sudden, I heard a loud noise. I turned to see what it was and found myself pounding into a telephone pole. I didn't have my seatbelt fastened, so I went crashing into the steering wheel. I could remember feeling severe pain in my body. I remember a crowd of people gathering around. The police came. The ambulance escorted me to the hospital, where I laid for hours before I was treated with anything for the pain. I was told that they did not want to give me pain medication until they could determine my prognosis.

Of course, by now, I had found out that Andrew was hiding in the back of my car. The loud noise was him jumping up. The impact sent him flying through the front windshield. He had a nerve to come into my room to talk with me. His face was covered with blood from the windshield cuts. I didn't want to talk with him nor see him. A very close friend and my ex-husband, Harold, were in the room and told him to leave. I found out later that my ex-husband threatened him. Abusers never stand up to other men. That was the last time I ever saw Andrew, except in my dreams.

I dreamed about him for a very long time. The dreams were always about him coming and harming me. Even though I never saw him again, he had the nerve to call me on my job. He tried his old tactics. He tried to get me to reconcile with him. I truly believe that he is mentally ill or just plain crazy. I told him that I never wanted to see him again nor talk to him. He never called again. However, for years, I looked over my shoulder. For months, I would check the trunk of my new car before I would get in it, for fear that he might be hiding out in it.

As a result of the accident, my hip was fractured. They repaired it with a metal plate and six, two inch screws. I was in the hospital for eleven days. In spite of my injury, the police officer had cited me for damaging public property and having no insurance. Therefore, before I could hardly walk, I had to go to court.

When the judge saw my condition, he dismissed the charges. I didn't have to pay any fines. That was a blessing.

I had to learn to walk again. It was a traumatic experience. I had never been sick nor had I ever had major surgery. So, this was a setback for me. In addition to that, I was an outside salesperson for Ivan Allen, an elite office supply company. As a single-parent, my job was my only source of income. I went back to work part-time within five weeks. Things would never be the same. I had a supervisor who seemed to be oblivious to my situation. He pressured me to get my sales back to what they were. Ultimately, I would struggle and end up losing my job. In this case, I believe that it was the best thing that could have happened, because it set the stage for me to get a Bachelor of Art Degree and a Master of Divinity Degree from Spelman College and Emory's Candler School of Theology, respectively.

"Chapter Seven"

"Reaching Abused Women"

I would like to pause here and speak to those women who are in abusive relationships. I would also like to reach out to those women who know women who are in abusive relationships. To the women in abusive relationships, be encouraged. To those who know women in abusive relationships, don't be judgmental. It's not as easy as you think to leave the relationship, as you have read from my experiences, which were even worse than you know, because I only shared bits and pieces of the abuse, abandonment and humiliation that I experienced.

First of all, the abuser never abuses in the beginning of the relationship. He usually waits until he has you "hooked" on his so called love. He does everything right, although there are warning signs along the way. Yet the abused person usually chooses to ignore those warning signs or red flags. We usually say, I'm sure he's not really like that; I know that won't happen again. Before you know it, your emotions are entangled in a web of lust, pain and humiliation. You say you can't take anymore, yet you continue in the relationship. Sound familiar? I know, because this is how I felt.

I would make up in my mind that I was going to leave. Then he would come with his tempting smile and seduce me into a situation that I really didn't want to be a part of. Nevertheless, the feelings get the best of you and you yield to the temptations. You feel wonderful for a moment and then the cycle starts all over. He abuses you again. For me, it went on for over five years.

I don't know how long you have been in your abusive relationship, but I do sympathize with you. However, you must pray and ask God to help you get out. It's not easy and even when you leave, it's not completely over. It's a chance you must take, lest you end up injured for life or dead. I know more than one incident where a coworker was in an abusive relationship and ultimately ended up dead. Don't let that happen to you. As I stated above, I could have been killed by him or in the accident that he caused. Abusers don't change, unless God intervenes. Most of the time the abuser does not want to change because it is a form of control. They usually are insecure and the only way they feel secure is to control someone else. They never stand up to another man, but only to a woman who is usually physically weaker, or just too afraid to fight back.

Please, for the sake of your life, find the courage to leave. I was very afraid. Even after I had made up my mind to leave, it wasn't easy. I came to a point in the abuse where I decided that I would rather be dead than to live in hell for the rest of my life. When I made my move, God made His move and the rest is history.

For those of you who know women in abusive relationships, reach out to them. Stop saying, "If I were you, I would or wouldn't …." Unless you have been in an abusive relationship, you just don't know what you would or wouldn't do. Encourage them to leave, and don't judge them. Pray for them and offer solutions. Offer them a safe place while you're at it, even if you have to help pay for the safe place. Whatever you do, show them love and don't give up on them. An abused woman is very confused and sometimes can't think rationally. The one thing they need is someone who is thinking rationally. PLEASE, get involved!!!

I also admonish mothers and other caregivers to talk to their daughters about abuse. Let them know that it is not okay for anyone, especially a loved one to abuse them physically, verbally or sexually. Please encourage them to tell someone if these kinds of things are happening. I don't care who the abuser is. In these days and times, it could be a father, mother, sibling, relative, preacher, doctor, or teacher. It's usually someone that they trust. Let them know that love doesn't "hurt."

Chapter Eight
"Rescued"

God had a plan for me—a way of escape. He knew just what I needed to overcome the devastation that I had been through in my previous relationship. He sent my "knight in shining armor, my current husband of over 20 years. He rescued me from a living hell. Roscoe is nothing like the other men that have been in my life. First of all, he is the first man in my life who was living for the Lord. He is the first man in my life who is a preacher. He is gentle, kind and loving and has never raised a finger to harm me. He is also a good provider. Also, this is the longest relationship that I have ever been in. We have had to work at having a good marriage, but that is true with any marriage. Thanks to God, my life is nothing like it used to be. In contrast to "hell on earth", I now have "peace on earth" and a loving husband and family to share it with.

Helen & Roscoe: 1987

Chapter Nine

"A Mother's Burden"

My oldest son is trying to recover from being addicted to crack cocaine. Recently, he has been in two different rehabilitation programs. The most recent one had me really impressed. Terence was really accepting the program into his heart. He was abiding by all of the rules and really trying to face reality. On Father's Day, the church affiliated with the program was having friends and family day. The one who brought the most guests would win a prize. I believe they honored first, second and third place. Terence had been so excited about inviting his children, his sister and me. My other son lives out of town and would not have been able to come. Anyway, Terence had been very encouraging and we wanted him to win. On that Sunday, he had a total of seven guests and came in second place. All of us were very excited about Terence's accomplishment. The service was very nice, too. Afterwards, the church served dinner. We ate and sat around talking for a couple of hours. It was a blessing to see Terence doing so well. All of us agreed that this new program was just what the "doctored had ordered." I left reassured that Terence was on his way to recovery. Then a very disappointing thing happened.

The Thursday after Father's Day, I called to speak to Terence. I was informed that he was no longer in the program. I asked what happened, and I was given a brief description of what happened. The overseer informed me that he was tired of dealing with Terence's anger. My reply was, "Isn't that what recovery is all about? Shouldn't there be tolerance for that type of behavior? Now, I am not trying to uphold bad behavior, but drug addiction carries along with it a lot of baggage. Anger is part of that baggage. I never received the entire story, but the point is, after all that encouragement, Terence had dropped off the scene. After about a month and a half, I heard from him. He was in jail and had been sentenced to one hundred and fifty days in a drug rehabilitation facility. I am praying that things will workout for him.

Now let me give you some background about Terence. He was a very bright child when growing up. He was mischievous, but not a real serious problem in elementary and junior high school. When he got in high school, he began to be somewhat of a problem, but it was still nothing like what I would deal with after he became an adult. At sixteen years old, his girlfriend got pregnant. He dropped out of school and joined Job Corps, so he could do the right thing concerning the baby. Terence grew up to be a nice looking young man, who is very intelligent and he can sing, too. However, he had some anger issues that began to cause problems. The bottom line is that at the age of around twenty years old, Terence got addicted to crack cocaine. He has been struggling with that addiction for the past twenty plus years. It has practically torn my heart out. When I was in the world, I was concerned about him, but it did not seem to bother me as much as it does now. As a child of God, my spirit grieves over his situation. I have watched him go in and out of several recovery programs. I have carried him food and clothing when he was homeless. I have rejected him and been hostile toward him. I have let him live with me and my husband (his stepfather) at least five different times. I have paid for him to live somewhere else when my husband said it was time for Terence to leave, because he wasn't trying to do better. I have prayed continually for his deliverance. I haven't given up hope, but I am now exhausted.

All of the things that I have had to deal with concerning Terence have really drained me spiritually, emotionally and physically. In recent years (from 2000-2004), I had not been physically able to do all of the running around I used to do for him. I had been in severe pain due to a hip injury from the previously mentioned automobile accident in 1987. My point is, my heart was aching and so was my body. I can't tell you how many days and nights that I have cried concerning my son. There is a saying: "When they are babies, they are on your lap. When they get older, they are on your heart." That statement is really applicable to my relationship with my son, Terence.

Moreover, what really frustrates me is wondering what makes him "fall off of the wagon" and go back to the "crack." There could be a problem or things could be going great. It does not matter. At the drop of a hat, he goes right back to the "crack." I just don't have the answer. I have turned it over to the Lord, but I still continue to pray for Terence. Another thing that bothers me is when I reach out to him, taking him clothing or giving him money. After doing those things, shortly afterwards, he usually disappears out into the "abyss" again. Now, don't get me wrong, it is not about the material and monetary things; it's about what it is that causes him to fall back into the same darkness. I just don't understand and I guess I never will. I do know that God is able to do abundantly, exceedingly above what we can ask or think. All things are possible to those who believe. I believe God can deliver my son and when He does, Terence will turn his "mess into ministry." For God showed me many years ago that Terence was called to preach. I guess that is why Satan has been attacking him most of his adult life. Nevertheless, "All things work together for good to those who are called according to God's purpose" (Romans 8:28). I am not giving up. Although the deliverance is not manifested right now, I am calling those things that are not as though they were. I am not waiting until the battle is over, I am shouting now!

Chapter Ten

"Caught Up"

The Georgia Lottery had its debut in the early 1990s. I really do not remember the exact year that it started. However I do know that in the beginning there were just jackpot games. Later on they would introduce Cash 3, then Cash 4. These would become my downfall. I got so caught up in playing the lottery that I couldn't function properly. Yes, by now I was a born again Christian. I didn't think it was anything wrong with playing the numbers. The bible does say we should not put our money to usury. But that refers to loaning money and charging someone interest on it. For me, the lottery was not in that category. Nevertheless, once something takes over your entire being and you are obsessed with it, whether it's a sin or not, you should stop doing it. In fact, it should never get that out of hand. Let me tell you my story.

When Cash 3 came out, I would play a number occasionally. It was not a big deal, nor was it often enough for any concern. After a period of time, I began to play more frequently. I started to think about it more, but it still had not reached obsession state. I used to play my anniversary date, 714. I had hit on it once or twice for $290 or $500. Then, in January of 1997, I won $2500 on 714. I was excited, but apprehensive, too, because my husband had told me that I shouldn't play the lottery. I did not listen. Well, once I won that large amount of money, I began to play everyday, trying to win big again. It's almost like a junky that takes the first hit and continues from that point on trying to feel that same sensation. From what I've been told, they never have that same feeling again.

Well, it took me a long time to win big again. This time it wasn't the same, though. I had been playing almost every day, to the point of obsession. The numbers consumed my very being. I would get up wondering what number would fall that day. I would play many numbers at one time. It was as if I were trying to play all of the numbers to ensure a cash return. After six months of continuous playing, I won $2500 again. Only this time it was from Cash 4, which started some time after Cash 3. At any rate, this time I had to go down to the Georgia Lottery Company because the winning ticket was over $500. Before when I won in Cash 3, I had five tickets for $500 each, so the local vendor could cash them for me. I went down there on my lunch break. I was very excited. Of course, for as much money as I had spent in a six month period, with only minimal winnings, the $2500 would not even make me break even. Yes, that's right, I had spent thousands of dollars playing the numbers.

It got to a point where I found two stores who would allow me to run a tab. I mean there was not limit. The devil really knows how to trap you. I would run up a big tab and when I did win, I owed it all to the store. It was sad, but I couldn't help it. By now, also, I was sneaking and playing the numbers. As I stated earlier, my husband said I shouldn't be playing the lottery, but I was "hooked," and didn't seem to have the strength to stop playing. Therefore, I would say that I was going to the store, which I did do. But instead of going to buy something that I needed, I was going to play the numbers. If you know anything about being hooked on the numbers, you know that you don't just go to the store, play a number and leave. There is an entire routine that goes with it. You go to the store, stand around and talk to others, decide what the hot number is for the day, play numbers, stand around and talk some more, play numbers, stand around and talk some more and on and on. So when I would get back home, I would feel guilty. I wouldn't actually lie, but I was being deceitful. I would spend so much time playing numbers that I couldn't concentrate.

This lottery saga took place while I was pursuing, get this, a Master of Divinity degree at Candler School of Theology. What was I representing? Who was I representing? How did I let things get so out of control? I was addicted to playing the lottery. I kept telling myself that I would stop. However, the next day, I would be right back at it. I would pray about it, too. But I didn't pray for God to take the addiction away. I prayed for God to let my number fall so that I could win money. I really believed that God would answer my prayers. Of course, now, I realize that God does not give us the things that are out of His will. The times that I did win were merely by chance. I would pray, "God please allow me to win big today. You know that I am in debt and the money will help me get out of debt. In reality, the money would have only helped me to continue playing the lottery, because I had not been delivered from it. It was a vicious cycle. I would spend large amounts of money playing the lottery, but

I would win small amounts of money, every now and then.

I remember going months playing every number in "triples" (000, 111, etc.). I had spent thousands on the triples. In the mean time, I was also trying to wean myself off of the lottery. So there would be times that I wouldn't play. I can remember this as though it were yesterday. As stated earlier, I had played the triples for months. I remember playing Christmas of 1997. I had played all of the triples, but I played triple fours about five times. They didn't fall. The next day, I was determined to stop playing the numbers, so I didn't play anything. Well, at 6:59 p.m., I was glued to the television. My heart seemed like it dropped to my toes when the triple fours showed up on the screen. I couldn't believe it. I was literally sick to my stomach. It was a big let down and I had to keep it to myself, because my husband was against it anyway. I called my friend, like I would always do when I would hit or not have the number that fell, especially if it were a number that I would normally play. You would think that I would have just stopped. But, oh no, now I was angry and wanted to get my money back. So I started back playing the triples and added to that the "quads" (0000, 1111, etc.). I played those from December 1997 until March 1998. I don't even know how I was able to continue in that vein, but I did. Of course, my tab was sky high. At one point, I had a tab of over $1200. One store had stopped allowing tabs. That really was to my advantage. The other store didn't stop. They would allow me to call my numbers in and go days without paying my tab. Of course, like I said earlier, when I did hit, I owed all or most of it to the store.

Then in March of 1998, I won $5000 on 2222. I was in so much debt by now that a large portion of it went to clearing out that tab. Another part went to catching up on bills, and yes, you guessed, I spent a large portion of it on the lottery trying to win big again. The vicious cycle was becoming a big dark hole and I was falling into it. I wanted to stop, but I just couldn't. Needless to say, I never hit big again. I would win here and there, but I spent it all back in playing the numbers. It got to the point where I would roll pennies so that I could play. As I look back at that phase of my life, I don't see how I functioned. Everywhere I looked, I saw numbers. When I was driving, the license plates would scream out at me—"play me; play me." I would buy number books, work out number puzzles, play dates, just anything to try to win that day. When I did win, it was to no avail, because I put it right back into the "business." There was no profit. It was as if I were running a business and putting all of my earnings back into the business, but the business was not thriving.

I was not thriving either. I knew that I had to make some changes, but it was so difficult. I had credit card debt, loans, and pawn tickets, all to support my habit. It sounds like a junky, right. Well it is about the same. No, the gambling didn't affect my physical being, but it sure played a number on my mental being. I became depressed. I knew that God was calling me into ministry, but I knew that I couldn't answer the call as long as I was addicted to the lottery. I did begin to pray for deliverance, but I would continue to play the lottery. I wasn't walking in the victory. I had let the enemy attack my mind. As you may imagine, I did very little things of the spirit, like studying the Word and praying. I had stepped out of fellowship with the Lord. I was an open target for the devil.

Things got worse. I spent more and more money playing the lottery and won less and less. I became anti-social. I just wanted to concentrate on the numbers so that I could win money and get out of debt. I know now that God had to turn my mindset around about money before I would be able to get out of debt.

But first, I would have to somehow start by stopping the lottery obsession.

In the meantime, I finally acknowledged my call to preach. It was December of 2000. I made the public announcement to the church. Even though I acknowledged my call to preach, I did not give up the lottery. As I look back, I thank God for His mercy during those dreadful times. I struggled more than one can imagine trying to overcome that addiction to the lottery. Keep in mind that I had been playing the triples and quads every day for months, plus many other regular numbers. I wish that I had all of the money that I spent on the lottery. I would be financially stable. Well, finally in February, 2001, I decided that I had had enough. The lottery was destroying me spiritually, mentally, emotionally and it was affecting my marriage, too. I remember going to the store that day. It was on a Friday. I would buy my last round of lottery tickets. I played all of the numbers in triples and quads, plus some other favorites. I played them for three days. By Sunday at 11:00 p.m., if none of the numbers fell, it would just be "too bad; so sad." I was determined to let it go and I did. Yes on February 3, 2001, I went cold turkey. I didn't win any money from those tickets, either. I know that it was best that I didn't, because if I had, I probably would have played again. I stopped playing, but the playing was not out of my system, yet. I would still have numbers rolling around in my head. I had to stop going to those stores where I used to play the numbers. Since then, I have occasionally gone to one of them to buy gas, but the one where they let me run up a $1200 tab, I have not been there since September, 2000. I had stopped going there months before I stopped playing the numbers. I didn't want to run up anymore tabs. So I had begun to break away before 2001, but I stilled played. At first, it bothered me when I would accidentally find out what number fell. My lottery buddy continued to call me and talk about the numbers even after I had asked her not to talk to me about the lottery. I had to eventually stop talking with her. Now, it doesn't bother me at all. Every now and then, the enemy tries to convince me that it's okay to play one number, just like he convinced Eve to eat the fruit. But I'm not buying it. I am strong in the Lord now and will not succumb to that temptation. I went through too much trying to overcome that addiction to ever again be entangled in that yoke of bondage. I like God's plan for my life. I am free and have an entirely different perspective about money because I started following the Spirit.

I deliberately made this a very detailed account, so that you could realize the impact that such an addiction can have on a person. You may not be hooked on the lottery, but anything that's not God's Word and consumes you, can be detrimental to your well-being. Seek God first and everything you need will come to you.

Chapter Eleven

"Going through the Process"

As I stated earlier, my right hip was injured in an automobile accident back in January of 1987. Once my hip healed from surgery, I was doing fine. There was no limp. I was able to walk and run, wear heels, and do those things that I was able to do before the accident. I did have to exercise some caution. Nevertheless, I wasn't physically challenged.

By now, I had remarried and things were going very well. As time went on, though, my hip started to progressively get more uncomfortable. The pain would be intense at random. In July of 1997, I had to go to an orthopedic surgeon to see what was wrong. I was told that over time, arthritis had set in and that was causing the pain. The metal plate was still in place, so that was not a problem. More time went by and the bouts of pain became more frequent. In June of 2001, I was in so much pain, I made another appointment to see an orthopedic surgeon. This time I saw the surgeon who would later do my total hip replacement surgery. He told me that my cartilage had worn and my hip area was bone-to-bone. In addition to that, bursitis had set in. Now I had arthritis, bursitis and no cartilage in my right hip. In essence, I was messed up and the surgeon told me that I needed a total hip replacement.

As a Christian, I believed that God could heal me miraculously. I prayed; the church prayed; many others prayed, but my situation did not get any better. There would be times when I felt comfortable, but it would not last long. I kept on believing God for my healing. I kept on praying, but there was no change. In fact, my situation had gotten worse. In June of 2002, I returned to the orthopedic surgeon. He gave me the same diagnosis, only this time, the hip had deteriorated even more. I still was not ready to have surgery. He had told me that he would not pressure me. When I was ready, I would come to him. He was right.

After continued prolonged bouts with hip pain, I finally decided that I would make an appointment for surgery. I was seeking God the entire time. I knew that God works through doctors, but I wanted a miracle healing. After all, God is no respecter of persons. Many others had been healed miraculously. Why couldn't I be healed without surgery? Well, God has a plan, and for me the plan was to take me through a process. My miracle would come in the recovery.

In January of 2004, I made an appointment to have total hip replacement surgery. I scheduled it for May 24, 2004. I waited that long so that I could fulfill my obligation to Georgia Perimeter College where I was teaching. By now, I could not take a step without excruciating pain in my hip and back. I was also walking with a cane. Nevertheless, I continued doing the things that I had committed to do, along with my household obligations.

The closer the time got for my surgery, the more apprehensive I became. I had felt a comfort in my spirit about the surgery, but as the time grew nearer, fear was overwhelming me. I would pray and ask God to take away the fear and give me peace. I would confess the scripture, "For God has not given me a spirit of fear, but of power, and of love, and of a sound mind," 2 Timothy 1:7. That would help for a while, then, I would be fearful again. The night before my surgery I decided that I was going to turn everything over to the Lord. Once I did that, I was relieved and confident. With my husband at my side, I was ready for the surgery.

It was a painful process, but now I am completely healed. Each time I went back for my check-ups (2 weeks, 6 weeks, 6 months, 1 year, 2 years, and 3 years), the doctor was pleased with my progress. He said that my hip was perfect. I had the newest material—the ceramic hip. He called it the "Cadillac" hip and it was doing its job. Of course, I followed the doctor's orders.

I don't know why God chose to take me through the process rather than heal me instantly. I do know that my testimony encourages many people. I conclude that the reason I had to go through the process was to have a testimony to encourage others. God knows what He is doing. No matter what you may be going through, He is still in control. It has been over 3 years since my hip surgery. You would never know that I had hip replacement surgery unless I told you. There is nothing in the way I move my body or walk that would indicate hip replacement. So, I did get the miracle, but I got it God's way not my way.

If you need a miracle in your life, take it to the Lord in prayer. He may not answer the way you want Him to answer, but I assure you that He will answer. He may not come when you want Him, but He's right on time.

After all that I had been through with the hip replacement surgery, I had an automobile accident on February 22, 2005. All I could think about was my total hip replacement. Would I be re-injured? The next chapter gives an account of the automobile accident.

Chapter Twelve

"Miracle on 316"

It was a beautiful Tuesday, February 22, 2005. I had several errands to run before going to my evening class at Georgia Perimeter College in Lawrenceville. I got the car washed, did some shopping at Walgreen's and returned home filled with the memories of being in Hawaii. It was about 80 degrees and for February, that was unusual. Earlier, someone had said that I was really trying to bring on springtime. I was dressed in a flowered pants outfit—one that I had purchased especially for Hawaii. I had a flower in my hair, one around my neck and flip flops on my feet. In a nut shell, things were grand.

For some reason, when it was time to leave for my class, I couldn't seem to get out of the house. I usually try to leave about 3:00 p.m., but that day, it was closer to 3:20 p.m. before I could get going. I was rushing and the traffic was backed up on each expressway that I would travel—78, 285 and 316. It was hot and I was frustrated because of all the days for the traffic to be backed up, it would be today when I was already running late.

There was an accident on 78 and 285—a big part of why the traffic was not flowing. Nevertheless, I inched my way onto Highway 316. I was almost at my destination. I had six plus miles on 316, less than a mile once I got off 316 and I would be on campus. It was approximately 4:15 p.m. Despite the traffic, I had made good time and would arrive on time for my class. However, due to unforeseen circumstances, I never arrived for my 5:00 p.m. class on that Tuesday, February 22, 2005.

After being on Highway 316 heading east for about 5 minutes, to my amazement, a vehicle headed west on 316 came in my view. The vehicle proceeded to cross the grass median, head directly into my path and crash right into the front of my 1998 Mazda 626, like-new vehicle. I could see it happening, yet it was so fast that I could only brace myself for what would come next. I remember saying, "Oh my God, I am about to have an accident." With those words spoken, I felt the impact of the Honda Civic pounding into my vehicle, full force. I was pushed around, skidded to the end of the road and stopped short of falling into the ditch that separated the east and west sides of Highway 316. The horn blew, the airbags deployed and all I could think about was my right total hip replacement. "Would that be re-injured?" Would I have to start all over again and have another surgery?" It was enough to overwhelm me and send my blood pressure skyrocketing to 192 over 100 plus.

I remember sitting there trying to recollect what had just happened. I remember slowly removing my seatbelt and reaching for my purse. I could see smoke coming from the front of the car and I was afraid it would explode, so I began to move faster to get out of the car. If you could have seen the car without seeing me, you would have concluded that the person or persons in the vehicle must have been killed or severely injured. Yet, I was able to exit the car on my own. Even though I could feel my face burning and my entire body starting to ache, I knew that God had spared my life. It was a miracle!

This is how the car looked after the accident on 2/22/05

A young man came toward me and asked if I was alright. I told him that I was not sure. I was in somewhat of a daze. It was like a dream. He offered to help me across the highway to get me out of anymore danger. I later found out that he was the driver of the other car that was involved in the accident. The lady driving the Honda Civic hit both of us.

After crossing the highway and trying to pull myself together, I was able to get a better look at the accident scene. The vehicle that had been in front of me was now in back of my vehicle. The driver of that vehicle was able to get out of the car by herself, too. In my mind, I wanted to ask if she was okay, but I was physically unable to go to her.

In the meantime, I had the sense to call my husband, but was unable to reach him. Then I called Angel, my daughter. She panicked, but was able to pull herself together and call Georgia Perimeter College to tell them what had happened and that I would not be in class that day. She came to the hospital and drove me home after they released me. I finally reached my husband who went home to see about our granddaughter, Alycia. I told him not to come to the hospital, because they would be sending me home shortly.

The police responded in less than ten minutes. He asked for my driver's license and my version of the accident. He later came to the hospital and returned my license. I was not cited. When I picked up a copy of the accident report, I found out that the driver of the Honda Civic had been cited for failure to maintain her lane.

The ambulance came on the scene as quickly as the police had come. I was the only one escorted to the hospital in the ambulance. They put me in the ambulance and the first blood pressure reading was 192 over 100 plus. The paramedic had to take a reading three times before it came down to an acceptable level. By now, I could feel the pain all over my body.

My face was burning and I could literally feel it swelling. There was a chemical release from the airbags that had a peculiar odor. I smelled that odor for days before it went away. In addition to the smell, my face had broken out with a rash which made me look like I had the measles. Because of the swelling in my face, it appeared as if I had the measles and mumps.

When I got to the hospital, fortunately, they were able to put me in a room immediately. That was a miracle, too! I later found out that the hospital had been very busy all day because no other hospitals were taking emergency patients. People had been waiting for hours for a room so that they could be seen. As God would have it, my room was waiting for me.

They took x-rays of my chest and hip. They ran other tests, but there were no serious injuries. The angels of the Lord had protected me from serious injury. My right hip didn't even hurt. Thanks to God, there was no additional injury to my right hip replacement. The majority of my pain was on the left side. Yes, it truly was a miracle!

I was grateful that my injuries were not more severe, but I was still in a lot of pain. I was angry, too. I had just had hip replacement surgery in May of 2004. I had recovered miraculously from that surgery and was on a walking regimen of up to 3 miles a day, 4-5 times a week. The thought of being re-injured devastated me.

The recovery process was also devastating. I could barely move without hurting. I had to sedate myself with pain medication, in order to function. I began to question God about what had happened. Why me, Lord? Just when everything seemed to be going great, an automobile accident totaled my car and fell short of totaling my life. We had just returned from Hawaii a week prior to the accident; I was still "basking in the glow" of such a wonderful experience. When the accident occurred, it put a damper on the joy of the trip to Hawaii. I had to go from sharing wonderful, exciting stories about Hawaii to the devastating, painful story about the automobile accident. God is so good. He let me know that it was okay to ask questions. He comforted me and let me know that He protected me from more serious harm and that I would be alright in the end.

Even though I received the peace of God in my painful situation, I still had to go through a lot of changes with the insurance companies regarding the car being totaled, the rental car and other things that pertain to accidents.

While I was still in severe pain, I had to go through grueling times on the telephone with the insurance adjusters regarding the accident. Then it was the process of renting a car. Then it was the process of getting my belongings out of the wrecked car. Then I had to wait for the insurance company's decision about the car: Was it totaled or could it be repaired? My car was paid-off and still like new, so I was very angry that I would have to go through the process of replacing my vehicle.

Furthermore, the insurance company that I dealt with first was my insurance company because we didn't have the insurance information on the at-fault party until we got the accident report. Then I had to deal with the other insurance company. It was a nightmare. Many things went wrong and took several phone calls to straighten out.

I was inconvenienced. Even though the insurance was prompt about sending me the settlement for my vehicle, it was not enough money for me to purchase a car comparable to the one that had been wrecked. I did not want a car payment because my car had been paid off for almost a year. I wanted to enjoy not having that financial pressure. I settled for a used van that ended up needing many repairs. It had been over twenty years since I had purchased a used vehicle. I had forgotten the problems one could have with a used vehicle. Between the accident and trying to replace my vehicle, I had to rent a car for over a month. The insurance company only paid for part of the rental. So I ended up paying a sizeable amount for car rental.

Moreover, I had to go to therapy. I had to take pain medication which I had had enough of before my hip replacement surgery. I missed work and had to re-do my syllabus to compensate for the lost time. I had to eventually drive to Lawrenceville to complete the semester at Georgia Perimeter College. Although I took an alternate route, it was still frustrating. Every time that I went to Lawrenceville, I thought about the accident.

Not only did I think about the accident, but I was literally afraid to drive. When I first left the rental agency, which is less than two miles from my house, I was terrified. So, when it was time to return to teach at Georgia Perimeter College in Lawrenceville, I was petrified. It is over thirty miles from my house. Like I stated earlier, I drove an alternate route plagued with heavy traffic and many reckless drivers. Nevertheless, I still had to cross over Highway 316. Every time I did (twice a week until May 3, 2005), I wondered if I would get hit again. After my accident, I heard about several accidents on 316.

Yet, I knew that I had to get myself together and overcome the fear. I cried out to God, "Please help me. I know that you didn't give me a spirit of fear." Every time I had to drive, not only to Lawrenceville, but anytime I had to drive, I would repeat those words. Gradually, I began to have more confidence while I was driving. It was not an easy task, but I made it through to the end of the semester and no longer have to drive to Lawrenceville. The Lord has completely delivered me from the fear of driving, but I still have to be cautious because other people drive very recklessly.

Even though I am over the fear of driving, I still remember the accident. When I think about it, I still feel the pain. Additionally, I have two scars, one on my face and one on my upper left arm, that have not gone away after over three months. I have never had a permanent scar on my face or arm. I have always prided myself in taking care of my skin and I should not have to deal with scars this late in my life. I know that God cares about everything that we care about—even the scars. So I believe that God will take away the scars just like He took away the fear and pain.

As I reflect on what happened to me February 22, 2005 approximately 4:15 p.m., as I stated earlier, I remember the fear and the pain. Yet I know that things could have been much worse. I could have been killed. I thank God for sparing my life. I know that God has great things for me to do and I want to do them. Satan wants to kill me, not God. Jesus said in John 10:10: ". . . I have come that you might have life and that more abundantly." Satan meant it for harm, but God meant it for good. "All things work together for good to those who love God and are the called according to His purpose" (Romans 8:28).

Chapter Thirteen
"After the Pain"

I have had much heartache and been through many painful situations. Some of them were because of bad decisions. In fact, in retrospect, most of them resulted from a bad decision that I made. I have written this book to encourage those who may be experiencing similar circumstances. We do things for different reasons. I do not know why I allowed my emotions to dictate my life rather than to allow my intellect to be in control. I thank God for sparing my life, when I could have been killed. I thank God for patiently waiting on me to give my life to Him. I do believe that without God on my side, I would be nothing right now. I thank my mother for praying for me daily until I gave my life to Christ.

I thank God for giving me a wonderful husband and family to help share my happiness. As I stated earlier, we have been married for over 20 years. Below is a picture of the beautiful roses that Roscoe gave me for our 20th anniversary, 7/14/07. There are a dozen red roses and a dozen peach roses. I wish you could see the beautiful colors.

I still like the zebra print!

7/15/07

I have also included the account of my car accident to encourage others. Maybe you haven't been in a car accident, but you don't know how you will pay your rent or house note. Maybe you have a loved-one who is suffering and needs healing; maybe you lost a loved-one. Perhaps you have a child on drugs or your marriage is "on the rocks." Whatever it may be, I am here to tell you that God is no respecter of persons. What He did for me, He will do for you. Is there anything too hard for God? Just call on God and He will answer you. No matter what your problems, God can solve them. The Word tells us to cast our cares on Him for He cares for us. Once we turn it over to God, we must leave it there. God doesn't need our help. He is well able to do above and beyond what we can ask or think. Let God work a miracle in your life. "Seek first the Kingdom of God and His righteousness and everything that you need, will be added unto you" (Matthew 6:33).

Remember that God loves you. If you do not know Jesus as your Lord and Savior, then accept Him today. Romans 10:9 states, "If you confess with your mouth that Jesus is Lord and believe in your heart that God raised Him from the dead, you shall be saved." That's it! All you have to do is repeat those words with a sincere heart and ask God to forgive your sins. You now have eternal life with Jesus Christ.

Epilogue

As I look back over my life, I realize that I have come a very long way. I went from teenage mom to college professor to ordained minister. I am now contemplating the pursuit of a Doctor of Ministry, as well as starting a business.

Additionally, earlier I mentioned missing out on my Class of 1963 graduation from Withrow. Well, this year in October, I will participate in the Class of '63's 45th High School Reunion. I'm still a "tiger" (our mascot).

Remember the devastation I endured because I had to quit the Minstrels at Withrow High School? Well, now I do liturgical dance at our church. God is so good. Who would have thought that God would have put dancing in my spirit at such a late time in my life. I was almost 60 years old when I began to dance at church. "If you delight yourself in the Lord, He will give you the desires of your heart" (Psalms 37:4). My dad wouldn't allow me to dance; the school made me quit the Minstrels; but God came through for me and now I am dancing for the Lord.

In between the experiences mentioned in this book, I was able to get two degrees: a Bachelor of Art in Religion from Spelman College, earning a 3.96 GPA and a Master of Divinity from Emory's Candler School of Theology, earning a 3.72 GPA. Both schools are in Atlanta, Georgia. I was almost 50 when I earned my undergraduate degree, but that didn't hinder me from being awarded several honors and scholarships for my outstanding academic accomplishments.

During the pursuit of both degrees, I was raising my granddaughter, Alycia Edwards, the one whom I mentioned in my acknowledgements. In my junior year at Spelman, I started raising Alycia, who was 9 months old at the time. Additionally, I had 20 credit hours 5 courses), was working 30 hours a week, and very active in our ministry. I earned a 4.0 that semester and the remainder of my undergraduate semesters. In fact, I only got one "B" and that was in my sophomore year. I really believe I should have gotten an "A" from that professor, but she gave me a "B" instead; thus I graduated salutatorian with a 3.96 GPA.

Moreover, I was able to take trips to the Middle East (Syria, Jordan, and Israel) and Greece, as part of a summer travel seminar. Also, my husband helped me realize a dream when he took me on a wonderful vacation to beautiful Hawaii. God has certainly given me the oil of joy for the spirit of heaviness (Isaiah 61:3).

By the way, the scars that I talked about in the "Miracle on 316" chapter have disappeared. I have no side effects from the accident and I am happy to say, I hardly think about it anymore—*driving as usual*.

I've been through many trials and tribulations and I could have easily given up. I mean, I was abused, ostracized, criticized, abandoned, etc. I had lost all hope. But one day, I received Christ in my life and things began to change. Things weren't better over night; but now I had a more reliable source of strength—"I can do all things through Christ, who strengthens me" (Phil. 4:13).

It took courage to tell others about my life, but I felt compelled to do so in order for others to benefit from the mistakes that I made; and to give them hope that they can receive healing and deliverance from their dismal circumstances.

It is not easy to tell one's story, especially one like mine. Yet, there is deliverance in one's testimony. God has prompted me to share my story as a ministry-of-healing tool, and I have accepted the challenge. In fact, I am already contemplating a sequel. The second book will highlight the positive things in my life that resulted from good decisions and obedience to God.

As I continue to reflect on my life, I also realize that when I was in the "world," I was caught up with the "lust of the flesh, the lust of the eye, and the pride of life" (1 John 2:16). That is all the world has to offer. Since I have accepted Christ in my life, I am a new creation. Old things have passed away, behold, all things have become new (2 Cor. 5:17). That did not happen overnight. Even after I was saved, I struggled with things, as I stated earlier; however, I now have an advocate, Christ Jesus, who is there to help me overcome my weaknesses. When I look back over my life, I can truly say, "I have a testimony."

I have humbly shared my testimony with you; and as I continue to preach the gospel and meet people, I will continue to share my story with others. Remember, God has a plan for your life and it's up to you to "step into your divine destiny today! *God bless you!!!*